parents

parents

A Toddler's Guide

by Ruth Pennebaker
Illustrated by Roy McKie

Clarkson N. Potter, Inc./Publishers
DISTRIBUTED BY CROWN PUBLISHERS, INC., NEW YORK

Published by Clarkson N. Potter, Inc., 225 Park Avenue South, New York, New York 10003, and represented in Canada by the Canadian MANDA Group

CLARKSON N. POTTER, POTTER, and colophon are trademarks of Clarkson N. Potter, Inc.

Manufactured in the United States of America

Library of Congress Cataloging-in-Publication Data

Pennebaker, Ruth.
    Parents: a toddler's guide.

    1. Parent and child—Anecdotes, facetiae, satire, etc.   I. Title.
PN6231.P2P46   1986   818'.5402   85–29737
ISBN 0-517-56188-3

10 9 8 7 6 5 4 3 2 1

First Edition

For Teal

Contents

Introduction ....*viii*

PART 1: YOU AND YOUR FAMILY

1 ☆ Knowing the Tall Ones *3*
2 ☆ Stereotyping Your Tall Ones *12*
3 ☆ The Baby Blues *20*
4 ☆ You and Your Grandparents *29*

PART 2: PHYSICAL FUNCTIONS

5 ☆ Wordplay *33*
6 ☆ Whining and Dining *39*
7 ☆ Dressing, Bathing, and Bedding *44*
8 ☆ Toilet Training *51*

PART 3: SOCIAL INTERACTIONS

9 ☆ You and Your Friends *57*
10 ☆ Birthday Parties: Taking the Cake *62*
11 ☆ A Baby-Sitter's Nightmare *65*
12 ☆ Preschool Daze *70*
13 ☆ Travel Notes *79*

APPENDIX: WHERE TO GO FOR HELP *84*

Introduction

I F YOU'RE A toddler, it should be clear to you that life is unfair.

Parents are tall. They talk in complete sentences. They boss you around all the time.

You're short. Your vocabulary is shorter. You can't boss around anyone except babies—and who wants to bother with them, anyway?

Let's face it: There isn't any dignity in being a toddler. You may still be in diapers with sappy names like "Luvs" and "Huggies." At best, you wear those soggy horrors they call training pants.

You have no privacy at all. Complete strangers come up and ask you how old you are. The woman next door wants to know when you're going to lose your baby fat. And your parents hound you constantly about your personal habits.

You spend your days staring at kneecaps, your nights peering through the slats in your crib.

And then the final insult occurs: You hear the Tall Ones complaining about you. The "Terrible Twos" or "Turbulent Threes," they say. Contrariness, stubbornness, tantrums. Will it never end?

You notice them consulting friends and pediatricians. You watch them snatch a dog-eared copy of *Dr. Spock* out of the bookshelves and read it intently.

"It's just a phase," the Tall Ones reassure each other. This isn't fair. You can't talk well enough yet to swap parent horror stories with your peers. And there are no books to tell you how to live with Giants in *their* terrible twenties or turbulent thirties. Is it any wonder that toddlers invented passive resistance?

It's time for a little advice for those who need it the most. So, if you're one of the underclass who can see eye to eye with only a cocker spaniel, take heed. Here are a few tips to make it easier to live with your parents—and to get your own way.

Just remember: You know more than you think you do.

YOU AND YOUR FAMILY

★

1

Knowing the Tall Ones

t O UNDERSTAND THE Tall Ones, you have to go back to their childhood.

Most of them grew up in the Fifties. These were the days before designer jeans, color TVs, personal computers, and punk rock.

Their mothers stayed at home and baked cookies all

day and didn't even have law degrees. Their fathers got home from work in the evening and said, "Honey, I'm home" and "What's for dinner?"

No one had ever heard of quality time, superbabies, women astronauts, or Suzuki.

When they were young, the Tall Ones had to do long division without a calculator. They had no role models like He-Man, Big Bird, and Strawberry Short-cake. This led to peace marches and sit-ins once they got to college. It was called The Sixties.

The Tall Ones love to talk about The Sixties. You'll know when they're talking about it because their eyes mist over and they sigh a lot. If they get carried away, they may drag out old pictures of themselves.

There's Daddy, with hair longer than Mommy's and a scraggly beard. He's wearing beads and sandals. And Mommy, who looks like she hasn't been to Elizabeth Arden in months. She's wearing a splotchy T-shirt that reminds you of some of your artwork. "It's a tie-dyed T-shirt," Mommy always says proudly. "I made it my-self." (As if you couldn't tell.)

They may get even more worked up about The Six-ties. They may talk about chucking the house, the mortgage, the two cars, and the credit cards—leading a simpler life. Living off the land, maybe. Teaching you "real" values.

You immediately wonder what you'll do without the color TV and your 2T designer clothes. What about your application to a feeder preschool? And your cre-ative movement classes?

Wait. Don't panic. These fits of back-to-the-basics are short-lived. Within minutes talk will have returned to money markets, tax shelters, Bloomingdale's, and Saab Turbos.

Relax, kid. These are the Eighties. Even your parents know that.

PARENTS ARE OLD

tHERE'S NO ESCAPING IT. The Tall Ones are getting on in years.

Remember the last birthday one of them had? You could hardly see the cake for the candles.

And you've seen how awful they look first thing in the morning. Why, they can barely move—even when you pounce on their stomachs. Once you manage to harass one of them into fixing breakfast, what happens? The poor thing just slumps and stares into a coffee cup.

Because they're so old, the Tall Ones' memories are starting to go. They're losing touch with reality.

Remember all the times you've played hide-and-seek with them and they've forgotten to look for you?

They may try to claim they were counting to ten thousand instead of ten. Don't believe it for a minute.

You'll have to be patient with them, but firm. Speak slowly and deliberately, reminding them of which game you're playing. Insist they join in.

And you may also have noticed that the Tall Ones are going deaf. You find yourself making a reasonable request—a fifth bowl of ice cream, say—and you get no response. They look like they haven't even heard you.

This requires swift action. Repeat your request over and over, with rapidly rising volume. Punctuate it with shrieks if necessary.

You will find this technique is especially effective in restaurants and other public places.

Parents Are Unimaginative

You may have heard of studies showing that people lose their creativity and imagination after the age of five.

Big deal, you think. You don't need some stiff with a PhD to tell you that. All you have to do is look at your parents.

Here you are, making a collage of mashed potatoes, smashed peas, and squashed carrots on the dining room table.

And what do the Giants say? Anything about your great future in the arts?

No.

Just vocal gyrations about your boorish table manners and how food is meant to be eaten, not played with.

Treat these slights of your work of art with injured dignity. If you feel quite strongly about it, sweep your creation onto the floor with one grand gesture.

PARENTS ARE UNFAIR

IF YOU WANT to get a big laugh, someday, just check out what the Tall Ones are reading about you. Magazine articles like "A Mother's Confession: Why Do Children Have to Go Through the 'Why' Stage?" Or, "Should Your Three-Year-Old See a Psychiatrist? Ten Easy Questions to Tell You When to Put Him on the Couch." Or, "Take Time Out for Yourself: Don't Let Your Children Run Your Life."

It's too much. The Tall Ones spend most of their time running your life, anyway. The last thing they need is more tips on bossing you around. Besides, all the so-called experts who write that junk are Giants themselves. So naturally they side with your parents.

Even worse, the Tall Ones have double standards. You never see either of them lend their clothes or cars to anyone, do you? But they're always pushing you to let that dorky kid next door play with your best toys.

PARENTS RUN THE WORLD

AS IF YOU hadn't noticed, huh? But it may be more pernicious than you realized. In the United States, where everyone is supposedly equal:

★ Toddlers can't drive.

★ They can't vote.

★ They can't drink.

★ They can't go to X-rated movies.

★ They don't have credit cards or even credit ratings.

★ They have a 100 percent unemployment rate.

★ None of them holds a college degree.

You have no idea why the Tall Ones think you're dense enough to have overlooked these frightening figures.

And then they wonder why two-year-olds whine so much.

PARENTS DON'T REALLY WANT YOU TO BEHAVE

t HE MYTH THAT Tall Ones want you to behave has caused countless children to feel guilty over the years.
You know the feeling. It comes when you think you've thrown a few too many tantrums or a few too many plates.

But wait. Don't feel guilty for a minute. You're actually doing the Tall Ones a favor.

Notice how they seem to respect you more when you respond with a loud, firm "No!" to whatever they suggest. If they'd wanted a creature who didn't talk back, they should have kept on growing philodendrons instead of having you.

And think, too, about your parents and their social circle. You'd disappoint the Giants dreadfully if they didn't have horror stories on the trials of parenting to swap with their friends.

If you hadn't tried to lock Mommy in the closet the other day, what would she have to talk about? Or if you hadn't put Big Sister's pet hamster in the dishwasher, how could your parents moan about the cost of new appliances?

The Tall Ones would be losers in the game of one-upmanship. They'd be forced to say something lame like, "Well, little Mikey's just a doll. I don't know what all this talk is about the Terrible Twos."

Then everyone would think they were repressing or denying. Or, worse, that you were a dorky, boring child.

How could you do this to the Tall Ones?

You couldn't. So don't even try.

2

Stereotyping Your Tall Ones

★   ★
                ☆

*t*HE TALL ONES, when they're on another child-care reading binge, will start comparing notes on what kind of child you are.

"I think she's an 'easy' child," you'll hear Mommy tell Daddy. "Most two-year-olds throw more tantrums than she does. I read about it in *Spock*."

Or, "He seems to be a 'difficult' child," Daddy says. "But they're more creative than other children."

All of this is quite insulting, really. You seriously doubt that clowns like Drs. Spock or T. Berry Brazelton know anything about you. You wish they'd write something about "easy" or "difficult" Tall Ones.

In fact, it occurs to you that someone should categorize the Tall Ones. You know that all of them have things in common like being grumpy, of course. But they also have individual differences that fall into a few obvious categories. It's just that no child has ever exposed them before.

A few easy-to-recognize signs will tell you exactly what kind of parents you have.

Superbaby Parents

I N THEIR TWENTIES and thirties they were working on their MBAs and JDs, and trying to make a killing in the corporate and courtroom world. They were very competitive.

For a long time, no one had babies. Then the women started to talk about their biological clocks. "We've got to have a baby before it's too late," they told their husbands. But the Tall Ones were still competitive. So they decided to have baby geniuses.

Check your alphabet blocks. If your parents want you to be a superbaby, the letters on the blocks will be Greek.

Other sure signs include:

The music played in your nursery. It isn't "Sesame Street." It's Schubert.

Your parents read you bedtime stories by someone named Virgil.

You've been playing the violin for the past six months.

You already have your own personal computer with educational software.

Your parents worry that you're lagging behind John Stuart Mill when he was your age.

How to Please Superbaby Parents

★ If you want them to leave you alone so you can paint Magic Marker tattoos on the dog, just tell them you're going to your room to compose a sonata.

★ Demand they read you Shakespeare at bedtime.

★ Tell everyone you want to be a PhD when you grow up.

How to Drive Them Nuts

★ Tell them you'll go deaf just like Beethoven if you have to listen to his symphonies any longer.

★ Say you'd rather watch cartoons than read.

★ Refuse to be toilet-trained until you're four.

★ Tell everyone you want to be a manicurist when you grow up.

LAST WHOLE EARTH PARENTS

dADDY AND MOMMY both wear sandals, even when it's snowing.

You shop in a food co-op instead of the local Safeway.

The Tall Ones are vegetarians. This means you can't eat hot dogs. Most of the food you *do* eat is brown and lumpy.

Your birthday cakes are made out of tofu and bean sprouts.

Your parents never call you "sugar" or "honey."

Your first name may be Moonbeam or Granola.

Your car is a '66 Volkswagen van with a "Ban the Bomb" bumper sticker.

How to Please the Tall Ones

★ Inspect every bit of food you eat and demand to know if there's any sugar in it. Gag at the sight of cake or ice cream.

★ Ask them to leave you alone at bedtime so you can meditate.

★ Ask lots of questions about the Third World.

How to Drive Them Nuts

★ Demand Twinkies for breakfast.

★ Ask for toy guns for Christmas.

★ Tell them you want frozen food—just like all your friends eat. Demand they buy TV dinners. Demand they buy a TV.

★ Tell them you want to be a Green Beret when you grow up.

YUPPIE PARENTS

YOUR KITCHEN IS lined with pasta makers and coffee grinders and your freezer is stocked with *gelato*. Mommy and Daddy worry that the living room has too many earth tones and they fret about the family portfolio.

You can learn the alphabet just by looking at your cars. Especially letters like BMW and XSL.

The Tall Ones buy you shirts with alligators on them and jeans with names on the pocket. For your leisure time, you have miniature tennis racquets and golf clubs.

Daddy will tell you that on the day you were born he celebrated by getting you on a waiting list at the nearby feeder preschool. Mommy says she even took the day off from work.

How to Please Them

★ When you're at a restaurant, order Brie. Then tell the waiter you don't want it because it hasn't aged enough.

★ Grab the Neiman-Marcus Christmas catalog the minute it arrives. Make them read it to you every night instead of *Mother Goose*.

★ Ask how old you have to be before you can have a Brooks Brothers suit.

★ Ask a lot of questions about bracket creep.

★ Tell everyone you're going to be a venture capitalist when you grow up.

How to Drive Them Crazy

★ Ask them to take you bowling.

★ Tell them Velveeta is your favorite cheese.

★ Ask a lot of questions about the Third World.

★ Announce you're going to join the Peace Corps when you're twenty-one.

LIBERAL, NONSEXIST PARENTS

YOU CAN ALWAYS tell this type. Daddy spends a lot of time in the kitchen, cooking perfectly awful things. In fact, he may even be a house spouse. Mommy claims she can't cook at all. They say "his-or-her" a lot.

If you're a girl, you have toy trucks to play with. The Tall Ones tell you you can be a doctor or a lawyer and it's okay for girls to be aggressive. As a matter of fact, they look proud when you clobber somebody.

If you're a boy, you have dolls. Mommy and Daddy tell you it's okay to be nurturing. They also tell you to cry whenever you feel like it and that you can grow up and be a nurse someday if you want to.

How to Please Them If You're a Girl

★ Nag them for karate lessons. Go around the house slashing at imaginary opponents.

★ Announce you want to be a five-star general when you grow up.

How to Please Them If You're a Boy
★ Ask to take ballet lessons. Cry when they tell you that boys don't wear tutus.

★ Say you want to be a poet when you grow up. Either that or a kindergarten teacher.

How to Drive Them Crazy If You're a Girl
★ Beg for a Barbie doll with a wedding dress and trousseau for Christmas.

★ Say you want to be Miss America when you grow up. Or a Mommy.

How to Drive Them Crazy If You're a Boy
★ Demand a football and a toy rifle for Christmas. Tell the Tall Ones that dolls are girls' toys.

★ Say you want to be Rambo when you grow up.

3

The Baby Blues

✩ ★
★ ☆
✩

fOOLISH CHILDREN NOT only like babies but demand that their parents provide them with one. They nag until the Tall Ones feel guilt-ridden enough to do just that.

Never make this mistake.

Sure, an occasional infant visitor is all right. It's nice to have someone around who's even shorter than you are.

But how would you like to have one of these red-faced, squalling bundles around for keeps? You'd be pushed off center stage pretty quickly. Remember, if your mother's midriff starts to expand, your troubles are just beginning, kid.

BAD NEWS FROM THE TALL ONES

YOUR FIRST SIGN that something is seriously wrong is that Mommy is wearing baggy-looking clothes. She also spends a lot of time in the bathroom and lies around looking green. Daddy's acting funny, too. He fusses over Mommy a lot.

The Tall Ones begin to ask you weird questions. Things like "Wouldn't you like a little sister or brother, honey?" Somehow you get the feeling it isn't really a question.

Finally, they get up the nerve to tell you the grim news. A new baby, they say. They're so happy. It will make the family complete. New babies are so much fun . . .

You can't believe your ears.

You thought the old family was just fine. Why do they want to mess with it? And why do they want to ruin your life?

You've heard all the rumors at preschool. Parents get tired of their old kids so they just have new ones. And then they'll probably cart you off to an orphanage where you'll have to wear a uniform and eat bread crusts and gravy until you're eighteen.

And it will be even worse if they decide to keep you. Remember Andrew after his baby brother was born? He just sat in the corner at school and sucked his thumb for six weeks.

You can't believe the Giants have made this terrible mistake.

They're still talking. Mommy has a misty look in her eyes. And Daddy seems real proud of himself.

"But we'll still love you the same as we always have," Mommy says.

SOMEONE ELSE'S BIRTHDAY

mOMMY HAS BEEN cranky for weeks. All she's done is sit around, complaining about her weight, her ankles, and her backaches.

And Daddy. Have you ever seen such a nervous wreck? He cringes every time Mommy lurches through the house.

Frankly, you're a little relieved when they finally go to the hospital. They packed up that suitcase with all those nightgowns and went screeching out of the driveway.

Grandma has come to stay with you, and she's been baking cookies all morning. It's not too bad, really. Until she comes up with that batty idea.

"Why don't we go shopping so you can buy a present for your new little brother or sister?" she wants to know.

You can immediately sense this is part of a trend. No one will ever buy *you* presents again. They'll only buy presents for the baby. You have to snuff that idea right now.

Insist that she buy a present for you, instead.

After all, you're still an only child. At least for a little while.

POSTPARTUM DEPRESSION

YOU'VE ALREADY been to the hospital to see Mommy and the Bald Kid. And you've already suggested that Mommy should come home and leave the Bald Kid in the hospital.

But no one has paid any attention to you. And against your better judgment, they've brought him home. It's just as you suspected: Your life is in ruins.

Everyone is whispering and tiptoeing so the Bald Kid can sleep. You start running around, doing your Superman routine. (Remember—the one everyone thought was so cute a few months ago?) And what do the Tall Ones do? They tell you to cut out the noise.

Then the Bald Kid wakes up and it's even worse.

First, he starts screeching. Then Daddy has to change his diapers—which is frankly the most revolting sight you've ever seen. Then they feed him, and he spits up everything all over Mommy's sweater.

Then it really gets unbelievable. You know how the Tall Ones are always after you not to burp and to say "Excuse me" if you do? Well, now they sit around with the Bald Kid and pat him on the back until he lets out a really big burp. And they actually look pleased when he does it.

"Isn't the baby adorable?" Daddy asks you.

"Shhhhh," Mommy says.

Present Tensions

*a*s THE WEEKS go by, you're sick of having the house revolve around the Bald Kid. All he does is sleep—except at night. Then he screams bloody murder and you can hear the Tall Ones thumping into the nursery.

During the day, there's been a steady procession of visitors. They all carry packages wrapped in blue or pink paper tied with white bows. You always race to the door when the bell rings and hold out your hands just in case the present is for you.

But it never is. It's always for the Bald Kid.

To be honest, you don't see what he's done to deserve all of this. He's still in diapers and he can't even hold up his head. He has to be carried everywhere and he usually falls asleep when people are talking to him. But none of the visitors seems to notice. They don't even mention how his eyes are crossed. They just sit around and coo and talk baby talk.

After everyone is gone, Mommy usually puts the Bald Kid in his crib so he can sleep until nighttime.

Then she picks you up and tells you how you used to be a baby, too. And how everyone came to see you and bring you presents. If she gets carried away, she'll even drag out some photographs and claim the weird-looking baby in them is you.

You don't believe it. You were never that little or dopey-looking. You don't know what Mommy is trying to put over on you.

You start to tell Mommy that. But all of a sudden she gets up.

"The baby's crying," she says.

REGRESSIONS

i N BETWEEN FEEDING and burping the Bald Kid, the Tall Ones have probably been boning up on those child-rearing books again. They're worried because you and the baby aren't best friends.

You can take a fair amount of advantage of all of this.

What Spock and those other bozos say is that you should be regressing. That means they expect you to forget you're toilet-trained and to want to have a bottle again and hang around your crib all the time.

You might humor the Tall Ones and do a few of these things—just so they'll know you're normal. If they wonder why you can't remember to use the toilet, mention that the Bald Kid doesn't either. Then ask why all he does is cry and eat and sleep. And why don't they love you anymore.

At this point, the Tall Ones will feel guilty and start telling you how much they still love you even though babies take up a lot of time. They'll say how they hope you and the Bald Kid will be good friends when he gets bigger and stops lying around and shrieking.

You know that will never happen, of course. Frankly, you don't think the Bald Kid has much potential.

But you decide not to tell the Tall Ones. After being up every night for the past two weeks, they look bad enough already.

4

You and Your Grandparents

★ ★
☆

nO ONE HAS to tell you how to act around your grandparents. They will think you're wonderful no matter what you do. That's why they're called grand.

Track mud all over Grandma's white carpet and she'll marvel at your little footprints. Crayon on their linen tablecloth and Granddad will predict a promising future in the arts.

Their idea of a wonderful vacation is to take you to Disneyland or Six Flags and ride the merry-go-round over and over after three helpings of cotton candy. For five days straight.

They never quibble about your chocolate-smeared

face. In fact, Granddad usually rushes to get his camera because he and Grandma both think it's so cute.

(In fact, there are photographs of you all over their house. There's one of you when you were eight days old and one when you were nine days old. There's one of you at eighteen and a half months and one at eighteen and three-quarter months. You wonder how they used to decorate their walls and tables before you were born.)

Grandma's always certain the Tall Ones aren't feeding you well—so she begs to know what your favorite foods are. (When's the last time *they* did that?)

You can usually get a little leverage here with your parents. All you have to do is threaten to tell Grandma how they feed you fish sticks three times a week, and the Tall Ones will be on their knees pleading with you.

Another bit of advice. Some shortsighted children try hitting up their grandparents for toys and clothes. Don't bother. You'll get that stuff anyway, even if you don't ask.

Instead, your most frequent words around Grandma and Granddad should be "trust fund." Tell them how your little friend Megan's grandparents love her so much, they've just given her a trust fund.

Actually, if your parents have anything on the ball, they will already have coached you on this.

PHYSICAL FUNCTIONS

5

Wordplay

☆ ★

★ ☆

FROM THE TIME you were a little kid—a baby, really—the Tall Ones hung around your crib and made lots of faces and noises and talked baby talk to you.

Then, if you smiled or gurgled, they would go nuts. Frankly, they haven't changed much.

If you started talking before you were two, the Tall Ones went around bragging to their friends how precocious you were. They would haul you out at cocktail parties to lisp a few words for everyone, and Daddy would say, "Well, it's Harvard for sure for this kid."

MEOW!

But it's even worse if you haven't started talking by age two. The Tall Ones look worried. All their friends' kids are talking. Why aren't you?

You're tired of your parents trying to coach you all the time and to coax words out of you. What do they think you are? A parakeet?

You don't talk because you don't want to. Why should you? All you have to do is grunt and point and they get you whatever you want. Why bother learning other noises?

GIVING IN GRACEFULLY

IF THE GIANTS ignore your repeated whines and outstretched fingers—even though it's perfectly clear that you want a cookie—then you know they're playing hardball.

Well, maybe it's time to give in, you think. You're not going to risk a full stomach over a philosophical dispute.

Besides, the effect it has on the Tall Ones is pretty funny.

"Cookie," you say.

Mommy's eyes bulge out. "Frank!" she screams. "Frank! Come here!"

Daddy comes running in.

"Frank—she said 'cookie'!" Mommy says. "Cookie! Just like that!"

Daddy's face lights up.

"Cookie," Mommy says, smiling.

"Cookie," Daddy repeats.

You don't say anything. You're too busy eating.

THE GIFT OF GAB

Y**OU MAY THINK** that once you've said your first word, the Tall Ones will never bother you again. After all, haven't you already proved that you can talk?

Unfortunately, it won't be enough for them to recall that on July 24, 1986, you once said the word "cookie."

No. They'll want you to repeat it over and over, every time you want a cookie. Worse, they'll want you to learn other words. Then they'll get even more demanding and start badgering you to put words together and make things they call sentences.

This is so you can have meaningful conversations like the Tall Ones have:

"Hi."

"Hi."

"How're you?"

"Okay. How about you?"

"So-so."

"What'd you do at the office today?"

"Not much. What about you?"

Just think: After thirty years of practice, you'll be able to talk just like that.

ON STAGE

t HE TALL ONES can often be quite irritating when they want you to "perform" for their friends.

No child with a mind of his own should ever allow himself to be exploited. Only dorky children agree to be yanked out in front of visitors so they can recite some phrases and have everyone say, "Isn't that adorable?"

Refuse to cooperate. After a few lessons, the Giants will catch on.

Try this the next time Auntie Ellen visits and they drag you into the living room to show off your vocabulary.

"—and just listen to Freddie say how old he is," Daddy is announcing.

Silence. Stare straight ahead and look blank.

"He'll say it in a minute," Daddy insists. "Wait till he gets warmed up."

More silence.

Daddy laughs nervously. "Freddie," he says, "tell Auntie Ellen how old you are."

Look at Daddy as if he's lost his mind. Furrow your brow.

"Well, he usually talks nonstop," Daddy says.

"I'm sure he does," Auntie Ellen says doubtfully.

At this point, you can really finish the Tall Ones off. Pop your thumb into your mouth, suck it, and stare.

Naturally, the minute Auntie Ellen walks out the door you will feel the urge to rattle off a string of sentences and four run-throughs of the alphabet.

For some reason, the Tall Ones don't look as enchanted as they ordinarily do.

SMART TALKING

IN TIME, you will learn the most important words and phrases in a child's vocabulary. They are:
"No."
"It's mine."
"I didn't do it."
And, "He hit me first."

Timing, you will learn, is everything. It's not just what you say—but *when* you say it.

"I love you, Mommy," for example. This is a perfectly nice thing to say. But it's even nicer to say after you've broken a lamp.

Or, "Please don't hit me, Mommy." Said in a sweet, piping voice at the grocery store, this has been known to make all conversation skid to a halt. Notice how Mommy looks like she wants to drop through the floor?

CONVERSATIONAL ENDS

ONCE YOU HAVE reached the "no" stage, the Tall Ones may be a little less eager for you to talk. It's too late. You've now decided you love to talk.

And it gets even better when you reach the "Why?" stage. At first your parents will think it's cute and they'll tell all their friends about it.

Then it starts to wear on them. You'll notice they get tired of telling you why you have to go to bed, why they're going to work, why it's cold outside, why the goldfish died.

But your real moment of triumph will probably come some evening at dinner. After you've regaled everyone with stories about *Sesame Street* and sung a few songs, you will notice Daddy turn to Mommy.

"Why did we ever want him to learn to talk?" he'll say.

6

Whining and Dining

☆ ☆
★
★

tHERE'S SOMETHING ABOUT mealtimes that makes you happy. Maybe it's throwing your food across the room that's so much fun. Or smearing it on your face and hair. Or finger painting with it on the tablecloth.

You can push peas up your nose, dangle a hot dog out of your mouth, make your spaghetti wiggle like a snake, or hammer your mashed potatoes so they almost hit the ceiling.

Unfortunately, the Tall Ones don't grasp any of this. They have very rigid ideas about food.

They insist that you sit at the table when you eat instead of running through the house. They tie a nasty-looking bib around your neck. And they keep bugging you to use a spoon and fork instead of your fingers.

If you touch your food—just to see what it feels like, that's all—they say you're playing with it. Then you hear, "Jackie, if you don't stop playing with your food, I'm going to take it away from you."

If you weren't starving to death right now, you'd let them go ahead and take it away. If this keeps up, you'll be as crabby as they are at dinnertime.

But don't despair. You've simply got to throw them off base.

You need to do or say something that will astonish them so much that they won't notice that the dog still has better table manners than you do.

For instance, you should say "please" and "thank you" all the time without being nagged. The Tall Ones will be so thunderstruck by your progress that they'll be beside themselves. They'll think it would be petty of them to mention how you're dismantling the egg rolls or dangling moo shu pork into your milk.

After all, if you're saying "please" and "thank you" one week, you may stop peeling marshmallows the next.

EATING OUT

YOU KNOW THAT sometimes when the Tall Ones stick you with a baby-sitter, they go to fancy restaurants where the menu isn't even in English.

When you're along, though, they go to what they call "family" restaurants. This means places with cheap prices, hamburgers on the menu, screaming kids at the other tables, and waitresses who chew gum.

The first thing you have to do at one of these restaurants is make certain you're treated with respect.

This is a little difficult—especially when the hostess looks at you and both the Tall Ones and says, "Two for dinner?"

You must correct this kind of slight immediately. Tell her, "No—Daddy's with us, too."

Once you get to the table, the indignities will continue. The Tall Ones will try to wedge you into a high chair or booster seat. Refuse. It's demeaning and childish to sit on one of those things. Announce

you're going to sit on a regular chair, "just like Mommy and Daddy."

At this point, you're in good shape. The Tall Ones will probably ignore any behavior on your part short of mayhem. That's because you're surrounded by

other people. The Giants would die of embarrass-
ment if they started to correct your manners
and you threw a tantrum.

They can't threaten to take you to bed because bed
is five miles away. And it's a long walk to the front
door of the restaurant if they have to carry a screaming
child.

So settle back in your chair and rest your chin on
the table. Start to make a nice little pile of salt and
sugar on the tablecloth. Shred your napkin and put
it in your water.

By the time your food has arrived, you will probably
realize that you don't want what you ordered. What
your parents got looks much better. That's all right.
Just demand a share. If they ignore you, feel justified
in grabbing whatever you want.

Finally, be certain not to let the waitress take your
plate away before you've finished eating. Just because
you're not picking up the check, some of them
think they can do whatever they want.

If this happens, scream about how hungry you are.
If you're quick enough, yank the plate away from
the waitress. So much the better if your half-eaten
hamburger and French fries fly onto the floor.

Everyone in the restaurant will turn around and
stare at your table. The waitress will have to apologize
profusely and bring you a new hamburger.

Somehow, you get the feeling she won't pull this
trick again.

But somehow, you also get the feeling the Tall Ones
won't be bringing you back here.

Funny the way your family never seems to visit the
same restaurant twice.

7

Dressing, Bathing, and Bedding

★　　★

☆

nOTICE THE TALL ONES some night when you're kissing all twenty-six of your stuffed animals before you go to bed. You'll see that they smile and elbow each other.

"It's just a phase he's going through," Mommy says. "I read about it last week. All kids this age have a lot of rituals."

You kiss your last teddy bear and sigh.

As usual, the yo-yos who write those books have missed the obvious point: The Giants have a hundred more rituals than you do.

Think of what they do every day. They get out of bed, take a shower, dress, eat breakfast, go to work, eat lunch, come home, eat dinner, and go to bed.

Worse, they're always trying to get you to conform to their rituals. They're forever bugging you to get dressed or to go to bed.

You wish you could say it was just a phase *they* were going through. But you know it isn't. You know they'll be this way the rest of their lives.

DRESSING DOWN

VERY MORNING, the Tall Ones force you into some clean outfit. It's bad enough that they won't let you wear your favorite blue jeans (just because you crash-landed in a puddle yesterday). But the clothes they buy for you are a disgrace.

None of them has the slightest bit of dignity or sophistication. How would *they* like wearing overalls and sweaters with bunny rabbits and teddy bears embroidered on them?

Naturally, you'll have to insist upon dressing your-self—even though you will find that the Tall Ones are terribly conservative. Mommy looks like she's having cardiac arrest when you emerge in the morning with a red plaid shirt and purple pants. But don't let her talk you out of it. Studies have repeatedly shown that you will be a six-year-old washout if you don't exercise your creativity now.

What's even more humiliating is when the Tall Ones insist that you get "dressed up" for a birthday party or your grandparents' visit. Those perfectly hideous starched and ruffly outfits can make you look like Prince William or Little Bopeep—not exactly the im-age you had in mind.

If your verbal protests don't register, don't let it faze you. Wait until an opportune moment, then trip and collapse into a mud puddle. Funny how mud shows up so well on white.

COMING CLEAN

tHE TALL ONES are obsessed with being clean. Every chance they get, they will force you into the bathtub. But really, it isn't their fault. You know that if your days were as boring as theirs—shuffling papers and bossing people around—you'd stay as clean as they do. Fortunately, you have a more exciting life of falling off merry-go-rounds and rubbing dirt in your hair.

Baths are yet another example of the Giants' lack of imagination. Their idea is to dump you in the tub, scrub you, and whisk you out. What could be more boring? You find you have to improvise constantly.

First, no one likes to take a bath by himself, so insist on being surrounded by at least ten toys.

Then insist on lingering in the tub for at least half an hour. Ignore the Tall Ones' protests and whines.

At some point, the Tall Ones will begin to howl in

earnest. If you're having a particularly good time, just aim a nice jet of water straight at them. This is most effective when they're dressed to go out for the evening. Even if you miss, they will have to spend the next few minutes mopping the bathroom floor.

But finally one of them will decide enough is enough and will drag you out. If they're especially diabolical, they will begin to let the water out of the tub while you're still in it. An untold number of children have been sucked down the drain, where they were chewed up into little pieces by alligators. Don't let it happen to you.

Try to leap out of the tub before the Tall Ones grab you. This way, you will be able to soak the bath-

room floor even more thoroughly. Also, grab the nearest Tall One for a big, wet hug.

Look around you. It's a disaster of soapy puddles on the floor and toys dry-docked in the tub. Down the hall, one of the Giants is soaked and sulking.

Fortunately, you're neat and clean. You wonder why Mommy and Daddy can't keep a little more order.

BEDDING DOWN

m AKE EACH BEDTIME an event to remember. You might succeed so well that the Tall Ones dread it and put if off as long as possible.

Start out by ignoring every bedtime warning the Giants give. Pretend to be so engrossed in your coloring book that you can't hear a word they say. Wait until their voices start gathering decibels, then look up and ask, "Why are you screaming at me, Daddy?"

Pretend to be perfectly compliant when Daddy takes you by the hand and leads you to your room. At the last minute, jerk your hand away and start running around the house at top speed. (It's fun to see the Giants crashing after you.)

After you get tired of running, just collapse on the floor and go completely limp. Daddy will have to carry you back to your room. He will also have to put you in your pajamas, which is about as easy as dressing an overcooked noodle.

Once you're finally in your pajamas, start issuing demands immediately—and don't compromise.

Two storybooks.
A trip to the bathroom.
A glass of milk.
Good-night kisses for Mommy.
Being tucked in.
A little more milk.
Another trip to the bathroom.
Night light on.
Being tucked in again.

Once Daddy has left the room, be perfectly quiet for several minutes. That'll be long enough for him to get settled in his easy chair and begin to watch TV. Then start screaming and make a few more demands.

Don't let this go on too long, though. You need your sleep. After all, you have to be up at the crack of dawn to get the Tall Ones out of bed.

8

Toilet Training

☆

★   ★

Y EARS AGO, when the Tall Ones were short, kids used to be toilet-trained when they were about three days old.

Then all the doctors who write the Tall Ones' goofy books got really worried and decided no one should be toilet-trained before the age of two. They convinced the Giants that you would end up as a mass murderer if they didn't hold off.

What this means is your parents won't bug you about toilet training until you're two. But after that, it starts to get intense.

You'll notice the Tall Ones become especially jumpy when all their friends' kids are toilet-trained. You know then that your days in Pampers are numbered.

Pretty soon, they will have bought a junior-sized

potty. They'll put it in the bathroom and start telling you how "big" boys and girls use potties. They'll nag you to sit on it "just for fun." They'll put one of your dolls on it and pretend she's using it.

Even worse, the Tall Ones will invite you into the bathroom to watch them on the toilet. This perfectly wretched idea is suggested by a lot of those doctors' books. You can't imagine anything more unappetizing than watching Mommy or Daddy use the bathroom. It's enough to keep you in diapers until you're sixteen.

Besides, you like diapers. You can use them any-time—while you're eating, watching TV, riding in the car. And now the Tall Ones want to march you off to the bathroom instead. All the spontaneity is gone.

But somehow, you don't get the feeling you have a choice. You can tell by the look in the Giants' eyes that they're determined to have you out of diapers any day now. It's probably a losing battle—but you can still have fun with it.

First of all, announce one morning that you have to go to the potty. Notice how Daddy's eyes light up. He hasn't been so thrilled about anything in years. Next, insist that he join you in the bathroom. Once you're both there, just sit and jabber. Don't do anything else. After Daddy's sat there for a while, he will start to feel ridiculous and get impatient. Finally, he will give up and haul you into the living room.

At this point, stage a nice accident all over the car-pet. Whimper a little. Tell Mommy you told Daddy you had to go.

"Your turn, honey," you'll hear Daddy hiss to Mommy while he cleans up the mess. "You were the one who was so sure we should be toilet-training her now."

It's always best to announce that you have to go when you and the Tall Ones are in a public place like a restaurant. Even though the Giants are certain you're just testing them, no grown-up can ignore a child whining, "Please, Mommy, I've got to go to the potty." The accusing looks from nearby tables are too much for them to bear.

On your more generous days, you might even reward them by relieving yourself in the potty. When you return to your table in the restaurant, make certain everyone within shouting distance knows exactly what you did in the bathroom. An update on what Mommy did is also in order.

Other children have succeeded in driving their parents to the limit by taking wholeheartedly to the toilet. In fact, they like it so much they can hardly stay away from it. They wash their hands in it, stuff their toys down it, unloose an entire roll of toilet paper into it.

If you regularly flush your toys down the toilet, you will find that you can strike up a close friendship with the plumber. In fact, he may even offer to put you on retainer.

And what can the Tall Ones say? They're the ones who started this whole obsession in the first place.

SOCIAL INTERACTIONS

9

You and Your Friends

☆

☆ ★ ★

tHE TALL ONES are always worried about how well you get along with your peer group. This is because they don't want a toddler pariah on their hands. Or a future ax murderer who is remembered to have been a "loner" in preschool.

So they load you down with advice.

If your Tall Ones are pacifists, they will tell you to: "Be nice."

Or, "Share."

Or, "Don't hit."

You always sigh when they say things like that. Your parents simply don't realize what a jungle the playground is. If you went around letting the other kids hit you, you'd soon be battered and labeled a wimp. If you always shared your toys, half the kids at preschool would walk off with them for keeps.

It's even worse, though, if your Tall Ones are frustrated jocks.

If they see your future on the offensive line of the Seattle Seahawks or with a black belt in karate, they will always be telling you to "stand up for yourself" and "don't let anyone push you around."

You frankly don't need this advice. There's no way you're going to "stand up" to some of these kids. Like the ones who are always talking about "getting protection" or "hit money." But you know how to handle them.

Just let them know that your daddy will beat up theirs if they don't leave you alone.

Once Daddy has gotten a look at *their* daddys—the ones who have those pretty drawings on their arms and ride motorcycles—he probably won't mention standing up for yourself ever again.

PEERS AND SNEERS

t HE ONLY KIDS you really dislike are the ones adults
are so crazy about. They're the kids you love to
hate.

You know who they are. The "perfect children."
They almost always have names like "Saxton" or "Adri-
enne." If they have nicknames, they're never "Butch"
or "Sissy"—but always "Jay" or "Missy."

They never get dirty. They never whine or say no.
They are always charming around adults. Once toilet-
trained, they never slip.

All of which leads the Tall Ones to sigh dramatically
and say, "Why can't you be as well behaved as Missy?"
Or, "Jay spends four hours a day perfecting his arpeg-
gios—and you can't even carry a tune."

Frankly, it's not even worth your while to tell them
that psychological studies have shown that polite, well-
behaved children end up on psychiatrists' couches
or in the penitentiary for pushing heroin.

IMAGINARY PEERS

m OST TALL ONES will be quite excited when you first introduce an imaginary friend. They know this is a sign you are precocious and imaginative and they will get to brag to all their friends about you. They will ask you your friend's name, how old she is, what her favorite foods are.

After a while, though, the Tall Ones' excitement may die down.

They may balk at setting another place at the table

for "Dot." They may not want to kiss her good night or tuck her in. They may refuse to buy her presents or a ticket to the movies. They may even worry that you're schizophrenic.

If this happens to you, remember that imaginary friends are very important to your development. You will grow up to be placid and boring if you don't have one. So refuse to let Mommy and Daddy talk you out of yours.

One tactic to use is to ignore Dot for a while. The Tall Ones won't be able to resist asking what happened to her. When they do, just shake your head and say, "She died in a car wreck."

In this case, your parents will be beside themselves. They will worry that they have "killed" Dot and now you are scared they will kill you, too.

All of a sudden, you will find that they are talking about Dot all the time and how she really didn't die in a car wreck. They'll make a great show of good faith by giving Dot all kinds of presents and her favorite foods. Be sure to remind them that you and Dot wear the same size clothes and like the same flavor ice cream.

Let them keep this up for a while. In the meantime, if Dot unfortunately knocks over a few lamps or hits a few kids in the playground—well, that's how imaginary friends are.

And it just proves Dot isn't really dead.

10

Birthday Parties: Taking the Cake

★ ☆
☆ ★

YOU'VE ALREADY BEEN to five birthday parties this year. You've bought presents for kids who really didn't deserve them—and who had the nerve to keep them. Frankly, you can't believe how greedy some children are.

But now *your* birthday is coming up. Naturally, you expect a party.

The trouble is—as usual—the Tall Ones. They're so forgetful. You're certain they won't remember your birthday and they'll forget that you want a party more than anything else in the world.

In fact, they look a little sick when you mention having all your friends over for a big bash with cake and ice cream. They mumble excuses like how you're too young for a party and they're too old.

Well, this is one time you'll simply have to pull out all the stops. If you let the Tall Ones have their way, your first birthday party may be your Sweet Sixteen.

It might take several days of hysterical sobbing and tantrums, but the Tall Ones will probably come around. After all, they'll feel too guilty if they don't give you a party.

Not guilty toward you, of course.

But toward all the other parents whose houses have been ravaged by the birthday parties *you've* gone to.

PARTY TIME

P UT ON YOUR party hat and station yourself next to your front door. This will allow you to grab your presents from everyone as soon as they arrive.

You notice that some of the kids are quite selfish and don't want to give you your presents. In fact, three of them collapse in screaming fits at the door.

You also notice how relieved their parents look when they hotfoot it back to their cars.

Your Tall Ones, on the other hand, look a little harried. You should have known they were too old for this much excitement.

It's too late to reconsider, though. By now, Dickie and Laura have turned over the goldfish bowl. Mommy is mopping up the water and Daddy is trying to catch the fish. Mary has bashed her head against the dining room wall, and Kay has bitten Clarisse.

Daddy starts yelling that it's time for cake and ice cream. He and Mommy make everybody stop fighting and crying, and you all go thundering into the kitchen. You elbow everyone else out of the way and keep saying over and over, "It's *my* birthday."

The Tall Ones light the candles and everybody sings "Happy Birthday" to you. You sing along, too, at the top of your lungs.

Then you spray saliva all over your cake when you blow out the candles. And you get to have three helpings of cake and ice cream.

The best part, of course, is when you shred all the wrapping paper and examine your presents. You smile, looking around the table at all the other kids. Most of them are crying because all they got were a few lousy favors.

You look at the Tall Ones. They seem tired, but also a little misty-eyed. They take pictures of you and your presents.

You sigh. It was a lot of work to put this party together.

But it was worth it.

11

A Baby-Sitter's Nightmare

Y OUR TALL ONES may selfishly decide they want
to go to a party or movie by themselves. You
know what this means.

　　You're staying home with a baby-sitter.

Naturally, you let them in on how you feel. This is
no time for subtlety.

Grab Daddy's shirt and whimper, "I wanna go, too. I wanna go, too."

If he ignores you, it's time to escalate.

Throw yourself on the floor and kick and cry and howl. Watch the Tall Ones between screams to see how they react.

The truth is, they probably won't budge. It never even occurs to them that you might like to go to a movie, too. They never think about anyone else. Why do you suppose they call them the Me Generation?

Pick yourself up off the floor with injured dignity. Glare at the Tall Ones' kneecaps. March to your room.

It's time to decide how you're going to handle the baby-sitter.

SITTING PRETTY

*a*CTUALLY, NOT ALL baby-sitters are bad. And the best ones are easy to recognize.

For example, the old, dotty kind. You can identify her by her low black shoes and support hose. If you're lucky, she'll be nearsighted and won't even be able to see the clock to tell if it's your bedtime or not. Or she'll forget what time the Giants told her it was.

She may concentrate so hard on her knitting that she won't notice you're painting your bedroom purple.

Or she may fall asleep on the couch fifteen minutes after the Tall Ones have left.

In fact, you'll probably have the run of the house. You may not even want your parents to come home.

Equally good are some teenage girls. You'll know you've struck pay dirt when she races to the telephone to call her boyfriend in Hong Kong before the Tall Ones are out of the driveway.

Some of them will let you help them inspect the refrigerator. If you promise you won't rat on them, they may even split the food.

Even better are teenagers with boyfriends closer than Hong Kong. If they have visitors during the evening, you might find them awfully preoccupied.

SITTING WORSE

Unfortunately, the Tall Ones may have different ideas about what a good sitter is. So what do they do? They hire someone just like *them*. You know the type: bossy, no-nonsense. You can tell instantly she's going to try to run your life for the next few hours. Just like the Tall Ones, except she's getting paid for it.

You have to be clever with this kind of sitter if you're going to get the upper hand.

First of all, you might try a peace offering. Show her the chocolate cake on the kitchen counter and suggest that the two of you split it.

She'll probably say no. Worse, she'll forbid you to have any cake. This means you'll have to step up the warfare just a little.

You can try to shake her off your tail by offering to play quietly in your room while she watches TV. That way, you can report later to your parents that all she did was snooze in front of the tube.

If this doesn't work, you'll just have to badger her. Try to wear her down by demanding that she play hide-and-seek and ring-around-the-rosy with you. Keep the games going good and hard until she collapses. Then you can tell the Tall Ones tomorrow that all she did was sit in Daddy's easy chair.

Once she's sitting down, drag your favorite book

into the living room. Nag her to read it to you over and over. Ask repeated questions like "Where did the dog go?" and "Is the cat going to bite me?" Follow up all her answers with "Why?"

After an hour of this, she'll be eager to get you to bed. Remember that it's not a good idea to refuse. Act perfectly agreeable about it. But continue to hound her.

Say no, you don't have to go to the potty.

Brush your teeth slowly. Demand more toothpaste.

Insist on a special pair of pajamas that you both have to search all over the house for.

By this time, you may be so tired that you actually want to go to bed. But inspect the sitter closely. You'll notice she looks a lot worse than you do.

The next morning, you may hear the Tall Ones say the sitter isn't coming back. Something about how baby-sitting takes too much energy.

Maybe they should try to get that high school girl again, they'll say. Sure, she did make a few long-distance phone calls. But really, she never seemed as exhausted as this poor woman did.

Sit back and congratulate yourself. You've won another one, kid.

12

Preschool Daze

✩ ✦
✩
✦

WHEN THE Tall Ones start talking about how you need to be around other children, take heed.

This means they're going to enroll you in a preschool.

They will take you to visit several schools. You hate them all, of course. You're not fooled by all the toys and smiling teachers. You're certain they're really prisons. Your parents will drop you off and never come back. (You wish now that you hadn't broken their heirloom vase last week. You're certain that's why they're putting you in jail.)

Besides, you can see how guilty Mommy and Daddy look. No wonder—when they're abandoning their child to eat bread crusts for the rest of her life.

When they drop you off, you beg them not to leave you. You promise to be good if they'll just keep you.

They swear they'll return to pick you up that afternoon. But you know they won't.

Throw yourself on the floor and howl. Cling to the Tall Ones' legs. As soon as they've rounded the corner, you can pick yourself up and start to mangle some Play-Doh. But they'll never know that.

By noon, you're having a decent time singing and listening to the teacher read to you. You notice that the food at this place is better than it is at home. Also, there are more toys. And you have to admit that playing with five other kids is more fun than hanging around with the Giants.

By the time Daddy appears to pick you up at five, you've decided this may not be so bad after all. No matter. Pretend not to remember him. When you're asked—in a hurt tone of voice—"Don't you remember Daddy?" look puzzled.

At the very least, you're assured an evening's free run of the house.

KNOWING YOUR DAY-CARE CENTER

n OT ALL PRESCHOOLS are alike. You can understand your Tall Ones better by looking at the kind of preschool they've decided to send you to.

Here are some examples for you to consider.

The California-Style Progressive Preschool

In this kind of school, you will notice children hanging from the ceiling lights and having races across tabletops.

All the kids are allowed to do exactly what they want because children are naturally beautiful and creative. Adults have lost this natural beauty and creativity and should try to be more like children.

Hyacinth, your teacher, refuses to stifle your innate creativity or to deny your feelings.

This means that throwing things is good because it releases anger. Cutting up your clothes with scissors is also good. It means you value creativity over material possessions.

In fact, you will find that Hyacinth appreciates you more than the Tall Ones. Remember that collage you made out of three pieces of bubble gum? Your parents looked positively nauseated when they saw it. But Hyacinth thought it was "pre-Warhol."

Every day, Hyacinth gathers all the children into a circle so that you can relate to one another and share all your feelings. Some of the children never join the circle. But that's all right, Hyacinth says. They're sharing their feelings by ignoring the group.

All of this allows you more leverage with the Tall Ones. Tell them they're "stifling" you when you get sent to your room because of a tantrum. Refuse to clean up your room because you don't want to be "structured." (You don't have to know what either of these words means. Just remember the dark look Hyacinth gets on her face when she mentions them.)

The only way you can get into trouble at a progressive preschool is when you insist on playing games and try to beat the other children instead of cooperating with them.

Hyacinth will immediately schedule a conference with the Tall Ones and tell them she fears you are becoming competitive.

After all, she says, all children are talented. There's no need to compete.

The Feeder Preschool

All the children's Tall Ones wear dark pinstriped suits and carry briefcases. The children have names with Roman numerals at the end and nicknames like Trey and Octo. The baby-sitters have English accents.

Your teacher's name is Mrs. Brown and she tells you stories like "The Little Engine That Could." The story means that anyone can get into Princeton, Yale, or

Harvard as long as he or she tries hard and has enough pull, Mrs. Brown says.

You have creative play in feeder schools, but it usually involves learning the alphabet or building skyscrapers. You are surrounded by Picasso and Rubens prints and there is classical music in the background. Mrs. Brown occasionally reminds the class that Mozart was already writing symphonies when he was your age.

Sometimes, when you are learning numbers at school, Mrs. Brown will hold up a graph. She shows you where you all are on the graph. And she tells you to remember that you have only fourteen or fifteen years until you apply to Harvard. "Time passes quickly," Mrs. Brown says.

Unfortunately, being at a feeder preschool doesn't offer you too many advantages with the Tall Ones. The only real leverage you can get with them is to tell them that cleaning your room or going to bed early will interfere with your "study time." Drag around a battered copy of some boring-looking book and say you have to "read" it. Mommy and Daddy will be impressed enough to leave you alone even after they've discovered you're only tearing out the pages.

"She just loves books," they can tell their friends.

In fact, you sometimes think your parents are much easier on you than Mrs. Brown is. All they say about your horrible table manners is, "Your grandmother would die if she saw you eating like that." But Mrs. Brown says something like, "You can never eat at the White House with manners like that."

In fact, Mrs. Brown doesn't seem to be at all worried

about stifling your feelings or stunting your creativity. So you're surprised when she schedules a conference with you and your parents.

"Your child just doesn't seem to be very competitive," she tells the Tall Ones.

The Giants look disappointed and talk to Mrs. Brown about motivating you.

After all, Mrs. Brown says, all children may be talented.

But only a few get into Harvard.

The Low-Rent Preschool

Naturally, you should always make certain that the Tall Ones send you to the very best preschool. You have to watch them, though. Some of them may try to save a few bucks by sending you to a cheap place.

Here are a few warning signs that you are in a low-rent day-care center and must take immediate action:

★ Do you have a different teacher every week?

★ Does your teacher take more naps than you do?

★ Does she tell you to "read your own damn stories if you want story time so much"?

★ Do you have Cheetos for snacks more than three times a week? Does the teacher tell you that Wing-Dings are one of the "Basic Seven" foods?

★ Does more than one of your classmates talk about his daddy being "on parole"?

★ Does the teacher turn on the TV so you can watch cartoons for six hours of "creative playtime"?

★ Do the Tall Ones mutter about being afraid to park their car "in a neighborhood like this"? Have they already lost more than one set of hubcaps while they dropped you off?

If you see any of these signs at your day-care center, you have to set the Tall Ones straight immediately. Tell them outright that you refuse to go to a low-rent preschool. If they don't do anything but look embarrassed, press on. You've got to transfer to another school or your future will be ruined.

Report daily to the Tall Ones how much the teacher slept and how long she read *True Detective*.

Try to recall every dirty word you have ever heard and repeat all of them. Tell your parents that's what you've learned at school. Tell your parents' friends, too.

Memorize all the commercials you hear on TV. Answer any questions with "Coke is it!" or "You, you're the one..."

When your grandparents ask you how you like your preschool, don't say anything. Just start to sob.

It may take a while, but no parents will be able to resist this kind of pressure. Any day now, you'll find yourself in a progressive or a feeder preschool.

The funny thing is, you will probably miss your old school and all those stories about "Daddy jumping bail." You'll get tired of well-balanced meals and creative play. It's been two weeks now, and you don't even know what's happened on *General Hospital*.

13
Travel Notes
★
☆
★

ONCE A YEAR the Tall Ones start bickering about taking a vacation. They talk about lying on the beach or skiing down a mountain. Or visiting your grandparents for the holidays.

You promptly tune them out. Frankly, you're not that interested in where you're going. If you know the Giants, they're too selfish to take you to Disneyland for a solid week. Any other place they pick will probably be boring.

But that doesn't matter. What you're looking forward to is traveling there. You know that's where the fun lies.

BY LAND

tHE BEST THING about traveling by car is that you and the Tall Ones will be closer together for a long time. It's a lot of fun for the family to be together.

Unfortunately, your parents often get crabby. So you'll have to keep the peace, as usual.

The scenario goes something like this:

You've sat quietly in your car seat for the past two hours, eating crackers and drinking juice. You've already stopped at two McDonald'ses and three rest rooms. That was pretty interesting. And it's nice to be out on the road. But you're ready to arrive.

So you ask, "Are we there yet?" for the sixteenth time.

"Not yet," Daddy says. He's using his "patient" voice. "We won't be there for another three hours."

You sigh. Three hours? You're already bored to death. You look out the left window. All you can see are cars. You look out the right window. More cars. You look straight ahead. All you can see is the back of the Tall Ones' heads.

"Are we there yet?"

Neither of the Giants says anything. Daddy turns up the radio really loud. You sing along for a few minutes. But the music is pretty awful.

So you ask, "Are we there yet?" again.

Daddy turns the radio up higher.

"I want some more juice," you screech.

Daddy turns around and peers into the back seat, where you've emptied out all your crackers and spilled your first cup of juice.

"Good god," he says.

Mommy turns around to look, too, and almost hits a truck.

"Are we there yet?" you ask.

Again, no one answers. You decide it's time to change the subject.

"I have to go to the potty," you say.

BY AIR

UNFORTUNATELY, you don't get to travel in close quarters with the Tall Ones when you fly. But it isn't bad because you have so much more room.

In fact, there are lots of seats on either side of you. For some reason, other people on the plane seem to avoid sitting by you. You wonder whether this is a special section for children or what.

But that's fine. As soon as the plane takes off, you wiggle out of your seat belt and start to explore.

Daddy sometimes gets airsick, so you run to sit in his lap and stare up at him. You keep hoping he'll have to use the barf bag and you'll get to watch. You peer into his face and try to make conversation. "Are you sick yet, Daddy?" you ask.

You notice that people in other seats seem awfully interested. Especially the people who are sitting right in front of Daddy. They turn around and stare. Daddy looks even worse.

Finally, you get tired of hanging out with Daddy and start to poke around the rest of the seats. First you

take all the magazines and barf bags out of the pouches. Then you dig in the ashtrays to see if there's anything interesting.

The Giants are pretending to sleep, so you have free run for a few minutes.

You decide to walk around a little. You introduce yourself to all the people in the next row. Then you show them your new shoes and your teddy bear and tell them how you're going to visit your grandmother. After a few minutes, you notice they've all gone to sleep too. So you return to your seat.

Every time the flight attendant comes by, you order a Coke with a cherry in it. This keeps you busy for a while. But then you're ready for the real fun of an airplane—going to the bathroom.

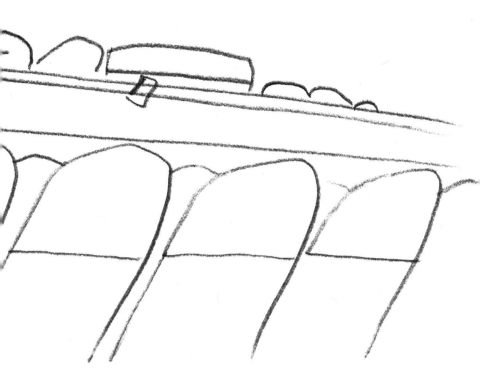

You have an especially good time today, because the flight attendants have to move the food cart out of the way for you and Mommy to walk down the aisle.

But it's worth the wait when you get to the bathroom. It's just as you remembered it: blue water in the toilet. It's beautiful. You almost hate to spoil the color.

Mommy soon becomes impatient and yanks you out of the bathroom. The flight attendants look a little grumpy about having to move the cart for you again.

But you don't mind. Thanks to all those Cokes you've been drinking, you know you'll be coming back soon.

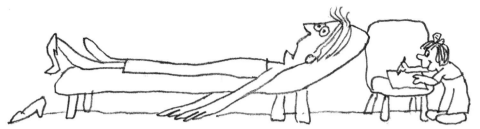

Appendix: Where to Go for Help
★ ★
☆

tHERE USED TO be nowhere to turn for children whose parents were driving them bananas. Fortunately, a nonprofit organization called Toddler to Toddler (TOT) has recently released a series of cassette tapes and records (78 rpm) to fill this gap. The series is entitled *The Terrible Twenties and Turbulent Thirties: How to Help the Tall Ones.* Tapes and records include:

★ "The Twilight Years: How to Humor Parents Past the Age of Thirty." Do your parents insist on thinking that they are young? Do they buy fancy sports cars and party dresses that are inappropriate to their age (and may rob you of a college education)? If your Tall Ones act like this, you need to help them come to terms with their age. This tape will show you how.

★ "Old Age and the Death of Creativity." Do your parents stand between you, your crayons, and a blank wall? Do they constantly nag you to "paint only on the paper, Jessica—and this time I really mean it"?

Senility may have robbed them of their creativity. Learn how to help them recapture it.

★ "Parent Talk." Do your Giants talk in the third person all the time? ("Mommy and Daddy would like you to stop making all that noise, Daniel.") A new study reveals that the tendency shows a lack of self-esteem. This tape will help you bolster your parents' egos (but not too much).

★ "The Body Is Beautiful." Are your Mommy and Daddy embarrassed when you drop your clothes at the door and run around naked? Do they constantly refer to your bodily functions with words like "pee-pee" and "poo-poo"? Then they have problems. You can learn to help them rid themselves of the sad inhibitions that often come with failing minds and aging bodies.

Order now. Tapes or records will be delivered to your house or nursery school in plain brown wrapping paper. Please, no CODs.